Money Problems & Solutions

Find Solution to Most Common Money Problems by Managing Your Personal Finance and Achieve Financial Success by Budgeting Your Saving and Debt

By: James John

CONTENTS:

Copyright

Chapter 1: Educate Yourself

Chapter 2: Trouble Saving Money

Chapter 3: Coping With Debt

Chapter 4: Don't Make Enough Money?

Chapter 5: Obstacles to Finances

Chapter 6: Healthcare Costs

Chapter 7: No More Debt

Chapter 8: College

Chapter 9: Bringing it all together

Conclusion

Copyright © 2016 by James John

All rights reserved.

In no way is it legal to reproduce, duplicate, or transmit any part of this document in either electronic means or in printed format. Recording of this publication is strictly prohibited, and any storage of this document is not allowed unless with written permission from the publisher. All rights reserved.

Respective authors own all copyrights not held by the publisher.

Chapter 1: Educate Yourself

Let's talk about money. Whether we like it or not, money makes the world go round. The economy that we live in is entirely based off of the usage of money. In a perfect world, there would be enough resources to go around for everyone, but unfortunately we don't. In fact, it's because of the imperfections of the world that scarcity exists.

The purpose of this book is to share insights into the various money problems that we can all face, and then look at the various solutions that are available. Make no mistake, when it comes to handling money it is very much a matter of living a good life versus living a difficult life. There are no exceptions when it comes to money. Having a good handle on your finances is a must if you want to be able to live well in this world.

Suppose you were speeding down a school zone one morning. The speed limit is 25, and you are driving at 50 miles per hour. You get pulled over by the police, and the officer says to you "Hey, you were going twice the speed limit! In a school zone!" What would the officer say if you replied "I'm sorry, I didn't know?" Do you think that such a defense would get you out of a very costly ticket? Of course not!

You might say you don't know the first thing about finances, that you might not understand the principles that make for good money management, but at the end of the day, you have no excuse when it comes to your bank account. Your money is solely your responsibility and that means your success or failure with finances is ultimately up to you.

Maybe you might feel that it is a harsh statement. Maybe you think that it is not fair that you have money problems or issues that have plagued you for a lifetime. But as long as you don't take responsibility for your decisions, you will never be able to grow past them. If you own up to your decisions that led you to the problems, then you will be able to start taking charge and start changing things for the better!

One of the most important parts of being able to navigate through your money woes is one word: education. Without proper education in finance, you will be forever guessing when it comes to your money. If you don't take the time, energy and effort needed to invest in your knowledge of fiscal responsibility, then any tip or piece of advice that you learn here will go to waste.

Education is the most valuable resource that you have in the war to take back your finances. Without a firm understanding of money, investment, savings and opportunity cost, you will not be able to secure yourself a strong and healthy financial future.

Regardless of your financial knowledge, there is some good news! You can get started on making good financial decisions right now by getting a great understanding of your own financial situation! Before we jump into the various money problems and solutions that exist, let's take a few minutes to review the basics!

Proper education of your financial future should be composed of three basic concepts:

Concept 1: Budgets

Your budget is your primary weapon when it comes to winning the war on your finances. A proper understanding of what a budget is will open the door to making the money that you want to make, controlling where your cash goes and ultimately empowering you.

Most poor financial situations stems from the improper application of a budget or even the lack of a budget at all! If you don't have a solid grip on how to handle a budget, then you are in serious trouble.

To gain a solid understanding of budgeting, you simply have to learn how to chart your money effectively. Some people prefer to use programs and spreadsheets, others like to write down in journals, tracking every expense by hand. No budget or poor budgeting is like planning to diet entirely off of eating whatever you feel like in the day. How many days do any of us feel like eating just salad?

Concept 2: Income

Money in and money out. If you don't have a proper education of how your money comes in and where it goes, you will be in almost as much trouble as not having a budget put together. Look at it like this; each dollar is a soldier in the war for your finances and if you don't know how many soldiers you have in the battle, then how will you know if you can win?

Simply put, one part in getting educated about handling your finances is sitting down and putting down every source of income that you have on paper. You've got to know what you're working with. Any type of income, put it down. You get $20 a month from your Etsy account? Put it down. You make $400 a week at your job? Put it down. If you neglect to account for all of your money that's coming in, you are not taking full control of your finances.

Money doesn't magically appear in your bank account and it also doesn't magically leave! Knowing how much you're making is equally as important as knowing how much you're spending!

Concept 3: Expenses

Finally, after you've budgeted and taken record of all of your income streams, it's time for you to focus on seeing how much money you spend each day. Note, we didn't say how much money you have budgeted, but rather how much you spend. For the next month, keep a log of every single spend that you do. If you spend a dollar, write it down. If it's 50 cents for the soda machine, write it down. Once you've sufficiently taken a log of all of your spending, check it against your budget.

Is it similar to how you've budgeted for the month? Many times it is not! This is the core problem in having money woes, that many times because of debit cards and quick, easy ways to spend cash, we become disconnected from how we spend our money. If you took a painstaking record of each dollar spent by hand each day, you will quickly see just how much money you have, and just how much you spend on a daily basis.

With these three principles reviewed, you should have a better grip on where your money is going.

But knowing is only half the battle. There will be much more discipline, energy and effort required to get to a place where you will be able to start dealing with the serious financial problems that plague many of us.

Chapter 2: Trouble Saving Money

Many a times the phrase is uttered "I can't save money, I don't have any" or "all those budget programs sound good but if I don't have the money, how am I supposed to save anything at all?" These are common reactions to the question of gathering savings.

It can be overwhelming when we think of all the bills that we must pay and then at the end of the day, we see that there is little left over to go into savings. Not only do we barely have enough to save, it seems that often enough, we don't have enough to have any fun either. It's either storing away money for later or spendingn it on enjoyments right now.

It doesn't have to be a war between saving your money and having fun. In fact, a good savings policy avoids dealing that problem all together. How? It's simple: a good savings program is one where you can achieve the goals you've set without having to think too hard about it. But before we get into a savings program discussion, let's look at the two major types of problem when it comes to savings.

Problem 1: Discipline

Savings is a discipline. There is really no other way around it. The process of saving your money isn't fun and it can seem to be way more beneficial to spend your money rather than save it. Long term, however, you will find that saving money tends to work out better for your health, bank account and financial wellbeing. It is possible that the money you are spending on frivolity or excess could be going into your savings account instead.

Ask yourself as you evaluate your savings: if I cut all spending on eating out, entertainment, alcohol and junk food, how much more money would I have? You might be surprised to find out how much you are spending in those areas. If that is the case, then you are dealing with the fact that your savings issue is a discipline issue. You are struggling to save money because you are throwing it away. The language is harsh and that is unfortunate, but there can be no sugar coating the situation.

The good news is that you *actually* have enough to put into your savings account - you just aren't. This problem can be corrected by choosing to prioritize your savings above fun expenses. This can be hard and will take self-control, a proper savings strategy and the discipline to stick to the plan but it will pay off in spades in the future.

Problem 2: Insufficient Funds

Perhaps you have looked at your expenses and you are barely making it month to month. This can be extremely problematic if you desire to save money up for emergencies, or if you want to have a cushion in case of unemployment or other short-term income loss.

So what do we do when we find ourselves living on a fine line between paying a bill and being unable to afford rent? It's simple, we learn to *hustle*. The spirit of hustling is desperately needed for the times in life where you find yourself living hand to mouth. Hustle involves making the active decision to start increasing your income stream by working incredibly hard to build up that stockpile.

There are many incredible ways to build up income through side jobs, freelance work, garage sales and focusing on figuring out how to make the most money you can. It will take sacrifice, working later hours, weekends and perhaps missing out on valuable social functions but the decision to build up that savings account will open the door for you to live with much more safely and securely in the future.

There are countless ways to make money on the side from your regular day job. You have many marketable skills and talents and in today's internet age, anyone can be a freelancer or entrepreneur. Finding work on Fiverr or other freelance websites such as Upwork can provide a steady side income, as well as crafting things and selling them on sites like Etsy. It might be harder work than one would want, but look at it like this: either you work incredibly hard for a great next month or you work incredibly hard for the rest of your life trying to make ends meet. Benjamin Franklin said "A life of leisure and a life of laziness are two things."

Before we move on to the next chapter, let's look at one of the most foolproof ways to build up on your savings account: automatic payments. The first step would be to have a savings account that is entirely separate from your regular bank account. You should not be able to easily transfer funds to your checking account with this speciality savings account. Rather, you should keep your accounts separate and once you have calculated how much you are able to save per month, set up an automatic deposit to that special account.

After you've set up your automatic payments and special separate savings account just… forget about it! Simple as that. Don't look at it, don't bother it, don't touch it. That money is as good as vanishing down a hole, at least until you reach your savings goal. By having a special place to place your savings that is out of the way, it will create a barrier to accessing and spending that money. Remember, 90% of savings is about having the discipline to put your money away. Once it's away, don't touch it *unless there is a serious emergency*. This will put you on the road to building up that savings account.

One last thought, even if you are only able to put $5 a paycheck away, please do it. $5 a paycheck in a month is $10 a month, which becomes $120 in a year. It might not seem like much but in a pinch, even $120 can be a real life saver.

Chapter 3: Coping With Debt

Debt can be a very crushing burden. When debt is present, we never truly are free as we would like to be. Debt takes a portion of our money per month and gives us back... what? Nothing. Debt is a problematic beast that can edge its way into not only taking over our finances but also taking over our lives. It can be worrisome, frustrating and worst of all, deeply stress inducing.

Debt is a tricky subject because once you have incurred significant debt, there is really no quick way out of it. There is only a steady, controlled method of progressive reduction to eliminate your debt and this will take a lot of effort and energy.

In order to figure out how to properly cope with debt, we must look at the various options and solutions that we have at our disposal.

Step 1: Calculate the total debt that you have.

In order to be able to properly tackle your debt, you must first calculate the amount of debt that you have, the different types of debt that you owe and the minimum payments required for each debt. After you've summed up each different debt and calculated the total amount of debt that you owe, you can move onto the next step.

Step 2: Consider ways to consolidate debt.

Credit card balances can often be transferred to other cards with lower rates. A car loan can sometimes be refinanced in order to obtain a lower interest rate. You might be able to take out a personal loan at a lower rate and pay off the remaining balance of your car. Looking into ways to reduce the interest rates on your debt is a great way to be able to reduce your total amount of debt by reducing how much you end up owing per month. Reducing rates means that you are reducing how much interest you are accruing on your debt and that means more of your money will go toward paying off the principal. The faster you pay off the principal, the faster you pay off your debt.

Step 3: Focus on the debts that you can pay off first

Once you have all the debts lined up and have done a good assessment of each one, choose only one debt to eliminate entirely first. Then, put as much free cash as you can (while still respecting your savings) into that debt. Try to pay it off as aggressively as possible, focusing as intensely as you can. It might not be easy but by paying off your debts as quickly as possible you are setting yourself up to have much more money in the future.

While paying off debt isn't fun, it's important to remember that debt isn't a joke. By taking control of your finances and paying your debt off as quickly as possible, you are opening yourself up to a better future. The trade off, unfortunately, is that you might have to reduce all excess spending for the time being, but the feeling of finally being free from debt will be worth it, we promise!

Chapter 4: Don't Make Enough Money?

As we look at the various problems that plague us in our finances, one of the biggest ones we can face, perhaps one even larger and scarier than debt, is the problem of not making enough money to live adequately. Sometimes our finances are in shambles because we are not making as much as we would like to. This can be a difficult situation. If you are trying to provide for a family of four on $12 an hour, you will have a very exhausting and frustrating time.

So what are the solutions when you simply aren't making the kind of money that you want to make at your job? Well, as we mentioned earlier, finding a side job can provide well in the short term, but if you aren't satisfied with working 70 hours a week just to make ends meet, what are your options?

Solution 1: Negotiate a raise.

This might be a little scary, but one of the more straightforward ways to make more money is to ask for more money from your employer. This might be intimidating but the chances of your boss saying no may be less than you think. Besides, the chances of you getting a raise when you don't ask for one is pretty low too!

So what's the best way to go in and ask for a raise? Well, first you need to know what your value is. Look at your job position, how much work you do and how much others in your industry are making. Come up with a fair and reasonable number and be prepared to show your employer all of your supporting data. If things go well, you might be able to either get a promotion inside the company or at least get paid a bit more.

This may go well, it might not. Some companies have policies based on giving raises, other companies may not be in the financial position to offer a raise, but if you have a good relationship (and a great reputation) with the company then it couldn't hurt to ask.

Solution 2: Find another job.

Job hopping may be looked down upon in the world and certainly you should maintain a certain loyalty to your company if they treat you well, but let's be really honest here: the moment you become a liability or unprofitable for your company, they will most likely let you go. Unfortunate, but that is the way that the corporate world works. They are inherently reliant on you working for them to make a relatively large amount of profit and in exchange, they pay you a stable wage. Once you stop earning them money for any reason, you will most likely find yourself looking for a new job.

Just as they have the ability to let you go at any moment when you stop being valuable to them, you have the ability to 'fire' your own company for not paying you adequately. This can sound strange but consider it. If you are unhappy with your pay at your job and unable to secure higher wages, what are you to do? If you have a limited skillset or a weak job history, you might have to be a little more selective with where you work but those who have good work history and plenty of skills shouldn't hesitate to look for a better paying job.

Looking for work when you have a job gives you the luxury to find one that will fairly compensate you. Don't be a mercenary though. Flying from job to job in the hope of finding something that pays you more might seem beneficial at first, but in the long run it can negatively affect you and your reputation. Just know that you don't *have* to work at a dead end job that's paying you poorly and going nowhere. You might have to be a little clever in your job search, but you are not obligated to stay at a job that isn't taking care of your needs.

Solution 3: Education.

Sometimes you have to choose to sacrifice more now so that you can have much more later. Going back to college to get a degree, enrolling on night classes at a trade school or getting licensed in a job might be just what you need to make more money in the long run. It won't pay off nearly as quickly as finding a raise or getting a better job, but investing in your future can lead to stable, fulfilling long-term employment.

Solution 4: Online Work

There are many solutions to your financial problems that can be found through making money online. It's just a matter of finding the right niche for yourself! There is money to be made through online sales of a product such as an eBook or arts and crafts, or perhaps you can make money through affiliate marketing or freelance work. Don't underestimate the power of finding additional income through things such as work from home transcription. An extra $20 a week is still an extra $80 a month which can turn into an extra $960 a year. That can easily go into your savings account or pay off some debt!

Chapter 5: Obstacles to Finances

Sometimes when walking through the world of finance, there can be obstacles that you will have to sort out in order to gain more control over your money. Most of the time, these obstacles can be in personal relationships or external circumstances. Let's take a look at a few different financial problems that can conflict with each other.

Obstacle 1: Family Problems

Perhaps you don't have trouble with your money, but your spouse is the one who spends the majority of your money. Maybe you are in a relationship where the checkbook is equally shared and you aren't seeing eye to eye on what your budget should be. Perhaps your children hit you up for money any time they need it and pass their irresponsibility with their finances onto you.

Relationships and money can be a very difficult road to navigate, especially when you are married or in a position where your partner(s) have easy access to your money. If you find yourself struggling with your money because your spouse or children aren't respecting your financial desires, then you must communicate what you want to achieve with your money.

Part of good financial leadership is walking the ones you love through your vision for a good, financial future and helping them reach the same page as you. Once everyone is on board with your plan to secure a great financial future and work through your financial issues, you will encounter significantly less financial problems. Communication is the key to getting your entire family working towards one goal: financial strength and prosperity.

Obstacle 2: Inappropriate Boundaries

A boundary is a fence or wall designed to keep people out. Boundaries are used many times when we say no to requests that ask too much of us, but sometimes when we have a poor sense of boundaries, we can have trouble saying no. How does that relate to financial issues? More than you think!

When we are able to confidently and strongly say "no" to others, we are able to have firm control on where our money goes. If a friend asks to borrow money and you know that he isn't liable to pay it back or has a terrible track record of managing his money, it would be ideal to say "no" to him. Having a good sense of personal boundaries will enable you to responsibly respond to those who might ask for your money.

Sure, there can be times when you are called upon to help others out with your money and there is nothing wrong with helping those who are in legitimate need, but make sure that when you are saying "yes" to others that it is out of a genuine desire to help, not from a feeling of obligation.

This might be a hard pill to swallow, but you honestly do not owe anyone your money. Many times relatives, friends or children can ask for cash expecting you to give it to them. If you are being put in a position where your own finances are being hurt to help someone else out, unless it's a serious emergency, then you should strongly reconsider assisting them.

Why? Because when you are unable to get on your own financial footing because others are inappropriately relying on you for assistance, you will never ever be in a place where you can freely assist them without having to choose between paying off debt and helping a neighbor pay a bill.

Getting your finances in order first is like putting your oxygen mask on first on an airplane. It will allow you to assist others after you take care of yourself. If you try to help others while you yourself are unstable, well, you can become severely injured!

Obstacle 3: Surprise Bills

Sometimes we can end up owing money without knowing it until the bill arrives in the mail. If you find yourself constantly surprised by unknown bills, unpaid doctors' visits or monthly charges that you can't remember signing up for, then you need to make a change.

First off, no bill should every arrive without you knowing about it in some way. If you find a charge that you don't remember, a doctor's bill that you were certain you paid off or a mysterious charge on your credit card, look into it immediately. Sometimes mistakes can be made and you never want to make payments that you don't actually owe.

Another helpful piece of advice is to have a bill schedule put in place so then you know exactly what day each bill is due and make sure you pay it on time. Paying late can accrue charges that will hurt you in the future. If you had the ability to pay but were late, then you're honestly just paying a "lazy tax." Make every payment that you can make on time every month and avoid paying outrageous fees that punish you simply for having bad timing.

Chapter 6: Healthcare Costs

Of the many kinds of debt to have, medical debt can be the scariest. Why? Because it's so incredibly high in the United States. When you incur healthcare costs, you can take on the average of over $1,000 just for an unfortunate trip to the Emergency Room!

Healthcare costs are moving up and up and for those who don't have insurance, an illness or a serious injury can be very damaging to your financial health. Fortunately, though, there are ways to navigate through the many serious costs of healthcare in the United States.

Option 1: Negotiation.

If you have incurred a significant health care cost for surgery, a trip to the emergency room or just a regular doctor's visit, don't accept any of their bills as law. Medical companies and doctor's fees are up for negotiation and just because they say you owe them $200 for a consultation doesn't mean that it's set in stone. If you have insurance then most of the negotiation will be handled by your insurance company, that's why they are there, but if you are uninsured, then you will have to fight your battles on your own.

First off, make sure you're speaking to the right people when preparing to handle a costly hospital bill or ER fee. It's no good to try and haggle with the doctor. There are departments within the medical care team that is meant to discuss finances.

Next, get a line item bill and be prepared to review each and every item. If your doctor won't itemize, that has plenty of potential for fraud, so make sure that each and every possible charge is listed. Then, go through the list and look for discrepancies, overcharges and prices that aren't acceptable or competitive with the area. These are the easiest to remove from the bill.

After you've prepared your objections, get in touch with the hospital administration and start negotiating over your bill. Make it clear that you are uninsured and that several thousand dollars of hospital care isn't acceptable for a broken arm. There are many more resources on how to discuss and negotiate with medical care providers online and if you find yourself needing to negotiate, you should look them up.

Remember, the bills you receive are not set in stone. You are entitled to receiving a fair bill for your healthcare and you do not have to pay just because they say it's X number of dollars. If you just roll over immediately without putting up a fight, then you are giving them money they might not deserve. It's on you to be diligent with your bills and to make sure that every charge is fair and accounted for.

Option 2: Charity

If you find yourself in a situation where you simply are not able to pay because of the sheer cost of the medical care, then you might be able to work out a charity donation from the medical care provider. Some emergency rooms will allow for this if you are below a certain income level and may write off your hospital bill as a charitable donation. Make sure you apply for these kinds of write offs or speak to the department in charge of such things and see if you can get even a percentage written off.

Sometimes, there are charities that may assist with medical bills. For example, a cancer charity may be able to support you with a small stipend or assist with obtaining low cost medicine if you get in contact with them.

There can be many resources out there that may be able to assist you with your medical care needs if you are unable to pay for expenses or medication. All you need to do is spend some time looking for the appropriate charity or in some cases, government program.

Option 3: Set Up A Payment Plan

As much as it might hurt, sometimes the only option with medical bills is to pay them and if you aren't in a position to be able to pay them what they want, you might feel the temptation to just skip out on the bill entirely or worst, pay it in full as fast as possible.

If medical debt is unavoidable, rather than jump ship or just pay it all off to be done with it, spend some time negotiating a payment plan that benefits you in the long run. Don't accept interest or if you are unable to get a zero interest plan, make sure that the interest is low enough to where it is almost negligent.

Make sure the payments are low enough where you are able to pay off the debt without any major upheaval in your life plans. It should be the last debt that you have to pay and you should be able to negotiate yourself into a position where it can be without any negative repercussions.

Medical debt can be a harrowing experience but by educating yourself and focusing on negotiating with the parties that you owe money to, you will be able to get a solid grip on your financial future with such an immense debt hanging over you.

Chapter 7: No More Debt

As we have looked at the many different ways to pay off debt and the various kinds of debt that can be incurred, let's look at one of the most important rules you can ever have when it comes to dealing with debt: debt is only for last resorts and living expenses.

It might seem like a tough rule, but the fact is, credit card companies are getting rich off of you for using their products to purchase things that you might not necessarily need. It can be very easy to obtain credit in today's day and age, and there is a constant push to purchase things with credit cards. The idea of getting something today and paying tomorrow permeates our culture, and as such, it can lead you down a road of incurred debt.

A hard and fast rule is that unless it's a car or a house, you shouldn't get any debt. It will prevent you from having to rack up thousands in credit card bills on things you might not need.

Debt only leads to more debt, and as you work to improve your financial status, there can be a temptation to take out even more debt to assist with bills in the short term. Resist this temptation, as hard as it might be and try to find any other way to pay off what needs to get paid off as opposed to going into even more debt.

Taking on debt to assist in your financial situation is akin to digging a hole in order to escape a hole. It will do you no good. There are no shortcuts in the road to financial freedom and stability and likewise, getting additional debt will only drag you down.

Making the serious decision to refuse to go into debt any longer may be difficult but will prove to be one of the best decisions that you can make in the long run. Having the discipline and the iron will to refuse to get what you want today and pay for it tomorrow will open the door to a strong and healthy financial future.

If you've found yourself struggling with unnecessary debt due to poor decisions in the past, leave those decisions behind. They don't have to dictate your future. As you focus on paying off your debt, cut up the credit cards once and for all and don't look back. A bad decision you made ten years ago doesn't have to follow you today.

In short, cut up the credit cards, save the debt for only long term arrangements like a vehicle and a home and *never* go into debt again!

Chapter 8: College

For some of us, we might be looking at going into the college system to receive a higher education. Others may be desiring to return to school or looking to get certification from a specific kind of trade school.

Schooling can be an excellent way to obtain a degree and knowledge in a proven field, but it can also be an extremely expensive decision. There are some colleges that cost over $40,000 per year, turning a 4-year degree into a $160,000 expense!

Not everyone has the kind of money lying around (I certainly don't) and looking at the cost of an upper tier school can lead one to buy into the idea that they might have to go into debt to go to college. This typically plays into the idea that a college education is a good investment and is worth the money but let us pause to actually consider this.

Many voices out in the college world advocate going into a large amount of debt under the assumption that eventually you'll be able to pay it back. This can lead you to believe that you will receive a specific amount of return for your investment immediately but this isn't true at all.

Just because you spend a large portion of money on a degree doesn't guarantee you any income on the same level, and so as an investment, it is not a particularly stable one. Yes, you will most likely be able to find a job with the right kind of degree but the problem occurs when you aren't able to keep up with your student loan payments.

Coming right out of school might not leave you equipped enough to pay off the entire debt quickly and with the way job markets are - a continual state of flux - you might not be able to find employment in the proper field. A large accruement of student debt can often give you some slack when it comes to wanting payment immediately, but the fact of the matter is, eventually you are going to have to pay it back and pay interest as well.

Now there are some times that student debt is appropriate, for example if you are interested in going into a very specific field that requires a lot of schooling and pays well such as a lawyer, doctor or financier. However, with the constant pressure that society places on the youth to go to school, you might find a history major incurring just as much debt as an accounting major!

It's important to keep in mind that college is an investment and should be treated as such. There can be times where investing heavily into your future is a good idea but you must consider all of the alternatives to spending a massive amount of college tuition before you make the plunge and go into debt unnecessarily.

Student Loan Alternative 1: Community College

For generalized degrees or getting your associates, going to a community college is an excellent way to cut down on the college cost! Most community colleges are significantly cheaper than a major university and many community colleges offer four-year degree programs. Instead of going for a costly degree for an Associate of the Arts, it may just be a better idea to pay for community college as you go along.

Student Loan Alternative 2: Scholarships

Don't underestimate the power of the scholarship! It can be an extremely valuable tool that can provide for funding. The only thing stopping you from potentially getting free money for school is not applying! Now, many times scholarships won't pay for the full amount of a college tuition but if you were able to even just get half of your expenses paid by scholarships or even just pay for your books, you would still be far better off than shelling out the cash yourself. Spending adequate time putting in the hours required to apply for scholarships can be massively beneficial to your bottom line.

Student Loan Alternative 3: Trade School

Trade schools teach valuable trades that often cost a fraction of college and give students important life skills that can be utilized immediately in the field. If you're primarily interested in securing a good financial future with immediate opportunities for a job, perhaps a trade school would work better than college. Trade schools impart practical experience that most companies look for nowadays and with the prices being about as low as community college as well as times needed to get certification or licensure being shorter, a trade school could potentially be the best investment you could make.

Student Loan Alternative 4: Working Through School

The last and probably most unattractive alternative to taking on student loan debt is choosing to work your way through school. Combined with scholarships and taking the cheaper college options that are available, working through school can assist you in paying off college as fast as possible. It might be more exhausting and labor intensive, but the payoff is worth it. Graduating from college with a brand new degree and zero debt can lead to a healthy and prosperous financial future!

Chapter 9: Bringing it all together

Ultimately with the many financial problems that exist in the world, it can feel overwhelming at times. Money is a very touchy subject and has caused countless fights, sleepless nights and emotional stress. Still, as you look through your own financial situation and take note of what needs to be handled, consider how enjoyable the future can be once you have sorted through your financial problems.

Changing habits, saving money and getting out of debt is very hard work and without a proper vision of the future, you can find yourself losing steam halfway through. This can be quite common and the cure for loss of enthusiasm is quite simply putting together a strong vision of what you want your future to look like.

Pause for a moment and seriously consider what you want your finances to look like five years from now. As you consider this, think about the fact that you, like everyone else, wants to have a financial life free from stress, frustration and irritation. The only way to get to this special place of financial security and freedom is to make the conscious decision to start working towards your goals.

Make a list of your major financial goals and place it somewhere that you can see every day. Work hard every single day to make this dream become a reality. You don't have to spend your time wishing for a better future when you can put in the time and energy to make for a better one today.

The stronger your vision is for your financial future, the greater the chance of you having the stamina and energy to put in the work. Don't ever think that just because you have made some bad financial decisions in the past that you are unable to make great decisions for the future. The only thing that is in control of your future is *you* and your habits.

You have the choice to make solid financial decisions, save your money and invest in your future. There is nothing holding you back from choosing that today is the day that you start working your way through all your financial issues, regardless of how overwhelming it might feel. Keep your eyes on the goal, develop a strong vision and don't give up no matter what.

And you'll find over time that as you continue to reduce your debt, increase your income and sort through the many financial issues that plague most households, that you're growing more skilled and capable of handling your money. The crazy thing about money? The better you are with it, the more you find yourself having. Now go out there and *hustle!*

Conclusion

Thank you again for downloading this book!

I hope this book was able to help you to improve your saving and spending habits by understanding money.

Finally, if you enjoyed this book, I'd like to ask you for a favor. Would you be kind enough to leave a review for this book on Amazon? It'd be greatly appreciated!

I want to reach as many people as possible as I can with this book and bring out the good strategies and ideas described to improve your money understanding.

Thank you and good luck!

DISCLAIMER: This information is provided "as is." The author, publisher and/or marketers of this information disclaim any loss or liability, either directly or indirectly as a consequence of applying the information presented herein, or regarding the use and application of said information. No guarantee is given, either expressed or implied,

www.ingramcontent.com/pod-product-compliance
Lightning Source LLC
Chambersburg PA
CBHW061223180526
45170CB00003B/1132